D1625353

# When
# I Am an
# Old Woman
# I Shall
# Wear
# Purple

Edited by
Sandra Haldeman Martz

PAPIER-MACHE PRESS
WATSONVILLE, CA

The poems, story excerpts, and photographs in this book
appeared in the original edition of *When I Am an Old
Woman I Shall Wear Purple*, edited by Sandra Haldeman
Martz, and published by Papier-Mache Press, © 1987,
1991 by Papier-Mache Press.

01 00 99 98 97  5 4 3 2

ISBN: 1-57601-052-X Hardcover

Photograph credits: Lyn Cowan, p. vi; Therese Becker,
p. 8; Lori Burkhalter-Lackey, pp. 16, 24, 32, and 40; Rod
Bradley, p. 46; and John Renner, p. 53.

http://www.ReadersNdex.com/papiermache

# Contents

# Warning

When I am an old woman I shall wear purple
With a red hat which doesn't go, and doesn't
   suit me.
And I shall spend my pension on brandy and
   summer gloves
And satin sandals, and say we've no money for
   butter.
I shall sit down on the pavement when I'm tired
And gobble up samples in shops and press
   alarm bells
And run my stick along the public railings
And make up for the sobriety of my youth.
I shall go out in my slippers in the rain
And pick the flowers in other people's
   gardens
And learn to spit.

You can wear terrible shirts and grow more fat
And eat three pounds of sausages at a go
Or only bread and pickle for a week
And hoard pens and pencils and beermats and
    things in boxes.

But now we must have clothes that keep us dry
And pay our rent and not swear in the street
And set a good example for the children.
We must have friends to dinner and read the
    papers.

But maybe I ought to practise a little now?
So people who know me are not too shocked
    and surprised
When suddenly I am old, and start to wear
    purple.

—*Jenny Joseph*

# Sitty Victoria

It's light. I sneak a peek from Sitty's bedroom door. She rises from the bed, bracing herself with blotched and shriveled arms. She sits in a giltwood armchair putting on her stockings, guiding an elastic garter up her swollen leg.

I walk through the back porch into the kitchen. Over the sink, through the open window, I see the morning come. A strange September morning. A loon in the air. The sky has taken on an eerie glow. I put on a pot of coffee, crack some eggs. Beyond the kitchen window an unusual morning wind turns suddenly wild, hurling leaves across the Summervilles' patio and against the side of their garage.

"*Sabah alkheir*, Sitty Victoria."

I bring her eggs to the porch. Sitty's sitting on the green sofa where she always sits. "*Ana bahibbik*, darlin'. *Inshallah nimti mnih*." She's always teaching me Arabic words, things like '*Allah maik*' and '*Allah yakun*'— 'God be with you,' 'God go with you.'

I catch the leg of a TV tray, slide it in front of her. I sit the breakfast tray down. Try to hand her an Arabic paper but she doesn't see me.

"Sitty," I'm on my knees, my face square in hers, "there's something I got to tell you, darlin'."

I touch her hand. It's cold. She's watching the wind bend the branches of a live oak next door. It's no use. I sit down, my arm touching hers, think about being stuck on that jet tomorrow. Think about a lot of things. How I've never been without her. How when I was a little girl, we'd pass the gardenia bushes by the Girl Scout hut at the Aurelia Street park where she'd take me swinging on clear April mornings and I could smell eternity.

—From *"Sitty Victoria"* by Vicki Salloum

# Like Mother, Like Daughter

"When are you coming?"
"On Sunday, why?"
"Because I want to get
some things, make the bed. . ."
"Oh, Mom," she said.
I felt an echo in me:
I had made the beds
just the week before
on a visit to my mother's,
because of her back.
Always before she had,
but now I did, knowing
where everything was:
I had moved her there.

Looking for recipes
of dishes my daughter likes,
I found the ones for meals
I had made my mother,
in her new kitchen,
and put them away
like an echo in a drawer.
Reviewing their ways,
looking for similarities
in their rhythms
(there were none);
I weighed them against
my need to be alone.

I am related to neither now
(their blue eyes are so dissimilar)
and yet I am their link.
There are echoes back
and forth through me:

I live alone, as do
my mother and my daughter,
none of us in the house
where we were raised or
spent our marriages.
Each of us is careful
of the others, unyielding
in small significant ways.

I now mother my mother
when I can no longer
mother my daughter
who is older than I
have ever felt myself to be.

—*Susan S. Jacobson*

# Near Places, Far Places

So there I was standing in my and Momma's dark kitchen looking at the light from Billy Walkingstick's cabin and the light from the moon that shone on the backyard and the flower beds and seemed to creep its way up toward me standing at the kitchen window. And up onto the presents from my grandbabies setting there on the windowsill.

I picked them both up, in one hand even, they were so small and brought them up close where I could see them good. They felt cool and I rubbed them against my forehead like folks like to do with a cold drink bottle. They still smelled like children do, sweet and sour at the same time. And they made my heart take a funny leap like I could have knocked down dead anyone who came in and tried to take them away from me.

Momma was right: You do have to get old before you do some thinking about some things.

—*From "Near Places, Far Places" by Sarah Barnhill*

# For My Mother

I sharpen more and more to your
Likeness every year, your mirror
In height, autonomous
Flying cloud of hair,
In torso, curve of the leg,
In high-arched, prim, meticulous
Feet. I watch my aging face,
In a speeding time lapse,
Become yours. Notice the eyes,
Their heavy inherited sadness,
The inertia that sags the cheeks,
The sense of limits that sets
The grooves along the mouth.

Grip my hand.
Let me show you the way
To revolt against what
We are born to,
To bash through the walls,
To burn a warning torch
In the darkness,
To leave home.

—*Michele Wolf*

# Birthday Portrait in Muted Tones

In this expanse of pale couches
and bone-colored carpet
the artifacts refuse to age. After
years of sun and heat, they still seem
like new arrivals popped from
cardboard cartons yesterday. The light
shining through the wide windows
make me giddy. I want to press
bowls and baskets down harder
on their tables, pound chairs
into the rug, give things weight.
My brother sits in what was
once my father's place. His hair
is grey like mine. Here
where we were never children
we rekindle old resentments over

the three-tiered cake. We are
the bad fairies at this celebration,
avenging slights. Our mother,
if she notices, gives no sign.
She smiles as we push our presents
toward her, picks intently
at the wrappings with slow-motion
hands. Reaching from my nearer seat
to help, I see how white her hair is,
bent over the stiff, bright bows.

—Dori Appel

# Late Autumn Woods

The press of green over
and the ritual of leaves

the wood has settled
into its prime dimensions
the lines etched in the light
pouring in from all sides.

Forts and nests abandoned,
the trash exposed.

Walking through
I can now see where the main
    path ends
and the others
branching off like veins on a leaf.

The palm of a hand
with a well-marked lifeline.
A wood thinned of possibilities.

Yet the sky, bluest in the north
and visible only in snatches before,
has opened up all around me,
as if a fog had lifted at last,
a heavy curtain.

—*Rina Ferrarelli*

# I Know the Mirrors

I know the mirrors
that are friends,
the ones in semidarkness that hide
the hard crease of jowl,
or the ones with the correct distance
to fade the barbed wire fence
above the lips. But skin breaks
like dry riverbeds.
Rooms must become darker,
distance greater.
I grope for a solution,
knowing that no woman
ever looked better with a beard.

—*Janice Townley Moore*

# Investment of Worth

You value the earthen vase—
    each crack applauded
    for authenticity.
a slave's Freedom Quilt—
    hand-pulled stitchery
    a rare tale relinquished,
Victorian silver hairpins
    with filigreed flowers
    delicate as unconscious.

A collector of ancients
       quite proud of your tastes
       but scornful of
              curled brown leaves
              slight grey webs
              parched desert soil
       of a woman
       turned and tuned to her ripening,
              whose life is dear
              as a signed first edition,
              whose death as costly
              as a polished oak bed.

—*Terri L. Jewell*

# words never spoken

walking through the city I saw the young girls
with bodies all silk from underthings to
   eyebrows
legs shaven
heels pumiced
nails glossed
hair lacquered
thighs taut
eyes clear
glad-breasted tittering girls

and I wondered how even for an hour
you could love a woman who has no silk
no silk
only burlap
and that
well worn
tattered
and frayed
with the effort of making a soul

—Doris Vanderlipp Manley

# Dear Paul Newman

After all these years
it's over between you and me.
There's a younger man.
I get to see him five times a week
and he tries to bring me the world.
I worried a lot about your racing
in them fast cars, your beer drinking,
the fact that the color of your eyes
is fading a little with age.
Them eyes always reminded me of Ed Kozelka
who sat next to me in American history.
When you and Ed turned them blues on me,
it sure made my pilot light blaze up.
When reporters asked why you was
faithful to Joanne, you once said,
"Why should I go out for hamburger
when I can have steak at home?"

Now that Joanne is looking so plain,
I wonder if you are going to Wendy's.
Paul baby, it was fun, and
I'll never forget your spaghetti sauce.
I gotta move on.
I'm the same age as you, but in the dark
Peter Jennings will never notice.

—*Marie Kennedy Robins*

# Love at Fifty

We come together shy as virgins
with neither beauty nor innocence
to cover our nakedness, only
these bodies which have served us well
to offer each other.

At twenty we would have dressed each
   other
in fantasy, draping over the damp flesh,
or turned one another into mirrors
so we could make love to ourselves.

But there is no mistaking us now.
Our eyes are sadder and wiser

as I finger the scar on your shoulder
where the pin went in,
and you touch the silver marks on my belly,
loose from childbearing.

"We are real," you say, and so we are,
standing here in our simple flesh
whereon our complicated histories are written,
our bodies turning into gifts
at the touch of our hands.

—Marcia Woodruff

# A Letter from Elvira

I saw your picture in the local news;
since you look like a nice lady,
I am writing you to find me

a princely widower, one who will appreciate
my three-college mind, the delicate lace
of my crochet, the gourmet taste of my
    cuisine.

He would need a house,
French provincial would be nice,
grey or maybe a forest green.

And a dog too, but not a boxer—
I don't like the way they look at me,
like these Methodists here in Baysville.

The preacher said I was reaching too high
and who would marry me anyhow. Some of
  them
are in drugs, the Mafia, you know,

and most of the Baptists are perverts.
The Board of Education is worse; they say
I'm too old to be teaching their children.

I enclose my picture, and my telephone
  number.
Have him call anytime; I'll be here.
I remain, yours very sincerely, Elvira Wade.

—*Bettie Sellers*

# Tin of Tube Rose

After *the change*, the children started growing up, one by one, and fending for themselves. For the first time in years, I had money for lipstick and dangling earrings. Why, I even bought myself a pair of fake eyelashes. Ed liked it. He liked it just fine. We joined the Moose Lodge and started going to dances on Friday nights. Saturday nights were extra special. While I bathed, Ed would look at pictures in his *Penthouse* magazine. Then we'd light the red heart-shaped candle that Sybil Ann, our eldest, gave us for Christmas.

—From "Tin of Tube Rose"
  by Sandra Redding

# Come to Me

Come to me looking
as you did fifty years ago
arms outstretched
and I will be waiting
virgin again
in white that changes
to splashes of roses
as we lie together
Come to me smiling again
with your mortar and pestle
and vitamin pills
because I am given to colds
and coughs that wrack us both
Oh come to me again
and I will be there
waiting with withered hands
gnarled fingers
that will leave their marks
of passion on your back.

—*Sue Saniel Elkind*

# Two Willow Chairs

"Now look, honey," she said,
"don't give up. Love is just a matter
of the right recipe: a cup and a half
of infatuation, a pinch of matching
class status, two tablespoons of
compatible politics, and three
generous cups of good sex. Mix.
Sprinkle liberally with the ability
to communicate and fold into a
well-greased and floured apartment.
You bake it for at least six months
without slamming the door and pray
you have love in the morning. And
it works—when you've got the right
ingredients."

—*From "Two Willow Chairs"
by Jess Wells*

# Planting

Two
Old people work
Side by side
She wears a hat
The old man boasts
No hair at all
She moves
And he kneels
He digs
And she nods while
He speaks
To the seed
She ardently covers
Row by row
They rise and bend
Over their garden
On earth
Sunflowers will bloom
Toward
Late summer

*—Cinda Thompson*

# Maybe at Eighty?

They say wisdom comes as you age
Now I'm in a real jam
At sixty I should be a sage
Look what a fool I am!

—S. Minanel

# Endurance

We women who have lived
through many winters
are sisters to mountain flowers
found in rocky crevices
high in the Alps.

Hardened by wind and snow
we endure cold
absorb brief sun
reach long roots
to meager sustenance
lift bright blossoms to empty air.

—*Fran Portley*

# Becoming Sixty

There were terror and anger
at coming into sixty.
Would I give birth
only to my old age?

Now near sixty-one
I count the gifts
that sixty gave.

A book flowed from my life
to those who needed it
and love flowed back to me.

In a yard that had seemed full
space for another garden appeared.
I took my aloneness to Quaker meeting
and my outstretched palms were filled.

I walked further along the beach
swam longer in more sacred places
danced the spiral dance
reclaimed daisies for women
in my ritual for a precious friend
and received poet's wine
from a new friend who came
in the evening of my need.

—*Ruth Harriet Jacobs*

# The Wildcat

I often dream of the wildcat. Usually I dream I come upon it by accident in the yard, or while in the pantry, or going somewhere in the car. One time, in my dream, I was awakened by its calling. It was early morning, the light was soft, the air pure, the day clear and inviting in a way I had completely forgotten a day can be. I stumbled from bed and down the stairs. The wildcat was on the screened porch at the back of the house. It was not so small, and it gave me a quick look of recognition—and then it took off.

I swung open the screen door and followed as fast as I could. The wildcat scrambled over the fence, and it wasn't until I was halfway over that I remembered I am seventy-nine years old and can no longer scale six-foot walls. Still, I kept looking over the fence.

—*From "The Wildcat" by Catherine Boyd*

# Social Security

She knows a cashier who
blushes and lets her use
food stamps to buy tulip
bulbs and rose bushes.

We smile each morning as I
pass her—her hand always
married to some stick,
or hoe, or rake.

One morning I shout,
"I'm not skinny like
you so I've gotta run
two miles each day."

She begs me closer, whispers
to my flesh, "All you need,
honey, is to be on welfare
and love roses."

—*Barbara Bolz*

# Out of the Lion's Belly

   She maintained that she'd had a marvelous sabbatical in Kenya, even in the face of those who were saying it had unhinged her and were calling for her dismissal from Lincoln Junior High School, where she taught art. These facts were undisputed: that before her year in Kenya, she had been a model teacher; she had been punctual, never arriving late to school nor failing to turn in her lesson plans in a timely fashion; she had graded her pupils' papers promptly and had been prompt for meetings with parents; she had promoted and achieved order, using only her softly modulated tones, never the shrill rage or the nasal sarcasm that were the modus operandi of the other teachers attempting to hold twelve-year-olds in check.

When the matter came to court, almost two years later, she again said, this time to the jury, looking past the shoulder of the interrogating attorney for the school district, that the sabbatical had been the highlight of her years, second only to the many hours she'd spent teaching Lincoln's junior high school pupils art, or, as she developed her notion, "those elements of art that would in some lingering way enhance and enlarge the vision of what in this life was important. Vision with a capital V."

"And did that year in Africa change your vision, Miss Inwood?" the attorney asked, pronouncing "Africa" as though it were a dark, vermin-infested cellar.

She blinked rapidly, cocked her head. "But of course it did."

—From *"Out of the Lion's Belly"*
  *by Carole L. Glickfeld*

# The Thugs

The years don't serve their time,
they're runaways,
they bump each other off
sun up, sun down.

Time, master mugger,
snatched this century
out of my hands
and fled.

—*Mura Dehn*

# Old Women

Old women
wrap scarves around their necks
to hide their wrinkles,
and flatter their bosoms
with bold beads and brooches.
In dresses buttered with flowers,
in voices light as baby's breath,
how they bloom in the corner
of the cafeteria, billowing
over pictures of grandchildren
passed round and round like hors
    d'oeuvres
like jewels they plant on each hand
to occupy the spaces once held
and warmed by husbands.

Now twined around each other
arm in arm down the sidewalk,
defying the dark grave
with their colors and perfume,
old women
tending time more fragile than youth:
poinsettias in the snow.

—*Barbara Lau*

# Words for Alice
# after Her Death

It came by surprise
like a blown fuse,
an old car you were used to
for a few errands, stolen.
We made room in our busy lives
to deal with your loss
as we had your illness.
You asked so little
I'm stumped with your elegy.
I'd rather rub your back
at your request,
or deal a hand of gin rummy.
At your own death you might
have let out one of your
high pitched sighs, your
reaction when landing on a chair,

shock of contact,
relief at getting there.

Now your old blue robe,
as familiar as the dark
green kitchen walls
will be in the last load
of laundry. The Fanny Farmer
box that held the savored
chocolate candy will
be emptied in the trash,
another act done
by one or two people
who kept looking in.

There won't be too much to move,
contents of closet, bureau, desk,
a bed and a few old chairs.
We already went through the pantry,
the spare room, eliminating
all but the nostalgic and necessary.

I find myself seeing your smile,
so welcome. It told of pain
for the time forgotten
in the pleasure of my brief company.
You were so grateful
for small acts of kindness
it was easy to feel blessed
for manicure, bed change,
buying a shower cap at the 5 & 10.
I see your white hair, eyes peeking
over the front door glass,
a blown kiss to assure me
you were safe inside,
but, frail package, how could
you be, really. That was
the old nurse's trick, to grin
and bear it, inquire about my health
first thing by phone call
in the morning. Yes,

you remembered my latest worry
and gave it an airing, before
we decided when I would see you.
I forgive you your resistances
to my consoling schemes—
for turning down good mystery books
because your eyes were failing,
for wearing the dress from India
only once, because the sleeves were tight,
and for picking at a Chinese dish
in a restaurant I had chosen.

Now I regret how little
your coin collection added up to
when I took it to the gold exchange.
The clerk said sometimes customers
salted the kitty for grandmothers
because they couldn't believe
how little their life savings

had come to. How little it all
comes to. But I used to remind you
at least you had interesting friends—
Buddhists and poets, an actor or two
and you agreed. And left alone
stains of fear and disease
on the sheets but didn't stain
our consciences with demands
we couldn't answer.
"What is the name of those beans?"
you wanted to know, embarrassed
to have forgotten.
I think I said every kind—pinto, string,
lima, green. But it was an avocado
that Jeff brought you,
on your mind. Hard to grasp,
like your bravery at the end,
trips down the old steps
to the washing machine,

outings in the car
to our affairs, picnic, rummage sale,
art show, when for you
a slow walk from bed to front room
must have seemed a trip to the moon.
It was no small feat
to heat up hamburger and add frozen
potatoes to the grease,
creating a great little Yorkshire pudding,
that left you pleased.
Your presence now is like the backrub
you tried to give me—the touch is
weak but gentle, and full of apology.

—*Angela Peckenpaugh*

# The Coming of Winter

The winter winds have chilled the warmth we
 knew
and whirl our unmet dreams like crumbling
 leaves
around the barren trees: a rendezvous
of weathered bones and somber dance which
 weaves
despair with sparks of hope that summon
 spring.
Beyond the wailing wind is sanguine sound—
the vigor-voice that wakes all  slumbering—
the reassuring call of power more profound.

We acquiesce to freezing winds and test
our mettle 'gainst the spectral storms ahead,
for there are forces that we can't arrest
and states of nature that we need not dread.
Beyond the winds lie gentler joys and peace
that sanctify our fate and death's caprice.

—*Shirley Vogler Meister*

# Post Humus

Scatter my ashes in my garden
so I can be near my loves.
Say a few honest words, sing a gentle song,
join hands in a circle of flesh.
Please tell some stories about me
making you laugh. I love to make you laugh.
When I've had time to settle, and green
gathers into buds, remember I love blossoms
bursting in spring. As the season ripens
remember my persistent passion.

And if you come in my garden
on an August afternoon
pluck a bright red globe,
let juice run down your chin and the seeds
stick to your cheek. When I'm dead
I want folks to smile and say    *That Patti,*
*she sure is some tomato!*

—Patti Tana

For more information about the writers or photographers in this abridged version, please see the biographical information in the original edition. For a catalog, call Papier-Mache Press at 1-800-927-5913.

*Design by*
*Linda Criswell*

*Composition by*
*Deanna Washington*